We Make the Path by Walking

Rejected Titles Include:

Read This Book, Billy Collins
I'm Sorry I Missed Your Wedding
Fish-sticks and Frozen Peas
Gnats, Gnats, and Gnats
Not Existential Enough
Expatriate
Armed Man on a Camel
Marked with Ash
Exile
Trust Your Feet
Shoe-rubber
Grit and Polish
Futility
A Strong Clutch of Flowers
Abrupt Narratives
Skeptical Dialectics
If All Else Fails

We Make the Path by Walking

Graham Robert LePage

For Sarah

Table of Contents

Traveler, there is no path.
We make the path by walking.
-Antonio Machado

Introduction

To begin,
I enjoy reading poetry.

Hopefully, if you are holding this book, you enjoy reading poetry too. I cannot speak for your taste, but I enjoy poems that strike the reader like a gong. I enjoy poems that have something significant to say. I also enjoy poems that joke around. I am not a stickler for form or free verse; both are fine, but I am skeptical about forced rhymes. I prefer poems that open the door for me and offer me a drink when I come to visit. I prefer poems, and poets, that sometimes talk about something other than themselves. No one enjoys a narcissist.

I started writing poetry before I began seriously reading poetry. I wrote because writing was a form of self-guided emotional therapy, easily accessible for a bookish and angsty teenager between cultures. But emotion does not good art make, and I wouldn't recommend those poems to you now.

It wasn't until I read poetry out-loud, faithfully, every week, with friends, combing through piles of books, that I began to enjoy poetry seriously. And now poetry has become a serious joy indeed. I have found that poetry, in the words of Garrison Keillor, makes you "buck up, pay attention, rise and shine, look alive, pull up your socks, wake up, and die right."

It is my hope that there is a greater density of poems in this collection that make you pull up your socks and die right. I cannot say for sure because I can only read them as their author, and what works for me may not work for you. What I hoped was a great brass bell of a poem may end up sounding cheap and tinny to your ear. But what I thought was a vase of plastic flowers, may seem, to you, a great cry of hope. One can never know with these things.

I. Chattanooga

Chattanooga

Chattanooga is a little city and a big town. The mayor calls it "the best mid-sized city in the United States," which is a very specific compliment. Others have called us the Portland of the Southeast, or sometimes the Boulder of the Southeast, which is all to say we are getting too cool to afford our own rents. We have craft beer, fried chicken, rock-climbing, BBQ, and internet so fast we don't know what to do with it.

Chattanooga sits on land stolen from the Cherokee, at the foot of Lookout Mountain, along a curve of the Tennessee River known as Moccasin Bend. Economic status and geographic elevation are closely related in Chattanooga, with most of the old money on Lookout Mountain and most of the new money on Signal Mountain.

Poor folks live in the valleys between the mountains. These lowlands used to flood periodically before the Tennessee Valley Authority dammed the river. The valley also used to be a good place to catch a fever from a mosquito. From my understanding, the rich folks weren't too fond of floods and fevers, and took to the mountains to escape. Nowadays, that historical inequality has become enshrined in Chattanooga's topography.

It was once a bustling, industrial, southern railroad hub with smog as thick as motor oil, and now it is a thriving, outdoorsy tech-town for tourists. The transition wasn't cheap or pretty, but the city is growing now. The turn-around has been dubbed "The Renaissance," a title which triggers anger in some folks. The reason being, if you were poor before the Renaissance, you are probably still poor now. The turn-around has been for the rich white-folks and the young professionals who are moving into town, but, for the most part, it hasn't included the poor folks. If anything the Renaissance has become a gentrifying force, pushing poor black folks out of the neighborhoods they have lived in for decades. That makes people angry.

I lived all over town: on Lookout Mountain, in a neighborhood named East Lake, in another neighborhood named Ridgedale, and in a satellite town called Flintstone. Lookout Mountain was shockingly charming and shockingly wealthy. East Lake was part Latino, part black, and part redneck, each demographic dealing with some level of poverty and gang violence. Ridgedale was a predominantly African American neighborhood where everyone was trying to hustle each other. Flintstone was a semi-rural "town" with its own isolated version of poverty and no real civic center. Your chances of seeing a Confederate flag increased exponentially as you approached Flintstone. And yet, each area is, somehow, part of the one thing we call Chattanooga.

Chattanooga is beautiful, kind, strong, rich, and hip, but it is also poor, violent, segmented, and inherently racist. To live in Chattanooga is to endure a great deal of contradiction.

Flintstone

I will hold your old men,
disabled and unstable.
I will give them pistols
and endless boredom.
They shall shop at the dollar store
for cans of refried beans.
They shall totter about the backyard
clipping brush to burn to smoke.
They shall walk on the shoulders of highways,
pushing a bicycle besides them.
They shall smile with rotten teeth.
You will see these things and say,
"What is man that I am mindful of him?
He is but a pile of leaves
scattered across the yard.
The wind blows and he is gone."

East Lake Evening

To what purpose
went the eight blue cop cars
so swiftly down my street?
The siren called out catastrophe
but it was a curious song
tempting me to follow after
and, doubting the deed,
to see the thing myself.
If I were to go and follow there
I would place my fingers
in the building's bullet-scars
pockmarking the brickwork.
I would collect one shard
of broken glass to keep.
I would place it on my tongue.
I would know good and evil.

East Lake Midnight

He was a short white man, my neighbor,
with a stout, square head
and the shadow of a mustache.
He enjoyed sitting on the front porch,
smoking stubs of blunts,
and sifting liquor with his liver.
We grew tired of hearing him
cussing out his mother
for telling him to quit smoking pot.
Perhaps, he was not a man yet,
though telling him otherwise
was not a possibility.
Really, he resembled a toad.
Was he kind? In his own way:
Friendly and talkative to a fault,
with a curious sense of honor
that demanded he start fights
with police officers
if they should ever, God forbid,
step on his foot.
The last time I saw him
was in the middle of the night
in the middle of the street
with a cigarette dangling from his lips
and his pants halfway down his legs.
His eyes glinted cheerfully
as he shook my hand and said,

"Watch yourself.
They're stealing
everything around here."
And he waddled away.

East Lake Morning

Chihuahuas roam the streets
as pit-bulls patrol chain-link fences.
It's a dog-eat-cat world out there:
brutal in its simplicity, with
unlit alleyways and possums
rustling in backyards at night,
clicking their short stubs of teeth.

But there are soft sides to this world:
the plump mourning dove's salutation,
the sudden red burst of a cardinal,
even the bright flash of chrome
as a gang-banger rolls by, they all
hint at something more
waiting behind all things
only ever glimpsed for a moment.

Even here among the payday loans
and flea markets, the fried chicken
and cheap gasoline, you might
suddenly catch your breath, unsure
of what you witnessed.

At the City Government

She is a skinny, old black woman with silver hair.
Her bowed and spindly legs barely support her
as she walks up to the reception desk.
There is a clear plastic tube that snakes
up her cheek and underneath her nose
to poke its little fingers into her nostrils.
The oxygen tank is of no more significance
than a leather purse. And today,
today she has all the necessary paperwork.
It is such an ordinary feat. Each day,
She rolls the boulder up the futile hill.
Tomorrow she may begin to forget, fading away,
but today she has all the necessary paperwork.
and has come to make her demands.

City Sidewalk

I am quite certain that
one day, while walking to work
my foot will break through the grate
that sits in its place in the sidewalk.
All of a sudden I will be hip deep,
one foot dangling, the other
straight out to hold me in place
for a moment before the grate
completely gives way and
my knee is driven against my nose
as I am forced through the hole
into the underworld beneath the sidewalk.
I do not know what is down there
where the false, warm wind blows
but soon, soon I will know
when I am driven down like a nail
and disappear into the city sidewalk
with only a brief grunt of astonishment
to mark my passing.

Overheard at Church

She said, " I'm going to cut him.
I'm going to give him one good cut
with his own knife. He is going to
give me his knife, and I'm going
to cut him. I'm going to cut him
so he can finally learn his lesson
and stop taking those damn pills."

4th Street

Biking past the homeless man,
I was ashamed that my bike
sparkled so blue and my jacket
was not stained or torn like
my other jackets.

Walnut Street Bridge

They poured money into downtown,
putting in bollards and new planks
to make the bridge pedestrian, accessible,
a walking bridge for the pasty-leg tourist:
the middle-aged white man in cargo shorts,
his wife in pastel capris. Perhaps
they didn't expect the dreadlocks,
the gang colors, the melanin,
the other citizens coming downtown
to enjoy those same summer evenings.
The police now patrol more often
ever since the shootings,
black boys killing black boys
under the very same bridge
that anchored the lynch-mob's noose.
"Who taught you to hate yourself?"

After Work

After work watching
the private despair of an old man
struggling with a gasoline pump
as though about to crumble
under its weight, and then
unable to step over the hose
to get back to his car. Hardly
enough strength in his hand
to squeeze the giant trigger.

Sawdust Lungs

Sawdust lungs can cough or choke when
menthol smoke slow soaks in crooked
teeth and ponytails. This redneck
nude to sun, though new to hope, though
crude by tongue; a country boy
falling down like thunder, rain, and
noontime naps from fast-food snacks with
work and beer and gasoline whose
fumes refuse to hide inside where
tumors grow and kill the lives of
those who live to live. Too bored to
live a life worth dying for, worth
loving more, worth living for. Cussing,
fussing, talking empty tank men.
They have found their paradise and
it tastes like a stomachache.

II. Covenant

Covenant

Covenant College lies on the grounds of an old hotel on top of Lookout Mountain. The hotel was built in the prohibition era as a pleasure castle, with rumors of secret tunnels to smuggle liquor into the basement. It was ultimately a failure as a business venture and was abandoned to the crows and clouds that haunt the mountain. It lay there as an Ozymandias of sorts until the 1960's when it was reclaimed by a small Christian liberal arts college. Covenant is the only college affiliated with the Presbyterian Church of America, a conservative and largely Calvinist branch of the Presbyterian Church that takes a great deal of pride in the adjective "Reformed." They tend to be precise in their doctrine, to take the study of scripture very seriously, and to place a lot of weight on the sovereignty of God.

I spent four years at Covenant studying poverty alleviation theory, micro-finance, international development work, poetry, economics, theology, and French. The college is surrounded by woods that hide trail-systems, cliff-lines, and caves. For whatever reason, Covenant seems to attract certain types of students: homeschoolers, missionary kids, hipsters, future pastors, barefoot granolas, North Georgian baseball players, Harry Potter enthusiasts, and soccer jocks. We are at the mercy of the weather, living on top of a mountain, and so many mornings in February are spent walking through a cloud, squinting your eyes, trying to find your way to class.

Every student at Covenant signs a contract to refrain from all drugs, alcohol, and sex while they are a student. This includes tobacco. Without any avenues for dissipation, the student body at Covenant can get bizarrely creative. While I was there, my roommates and I named our pet fish after dictators, (Stalin, Hitler, Mussolini, and Stephen Harper) and then read the poetry of Tupac over their graves when those same authoritarian fish died. Some folks staged a virgin sacrifice to the gods of spring whenever the college board was on campus. It was an elaborate piece of public theater that involved cross-dressing, electric guitar solos, and a real cow's heart, still dripping with blood. Needless to say, it made the board very uncomfortable. I once attended a dance party with a life-sized rhino puppet that stomped around the dance floor. The college chapel thundered with hymn-singing in the morning, the trees clustered with hammocks in the afternoon, and dubstep throbbed in the dorms at night.

Or at least it was dubstep when I arrived, but it was trap music thumping and rattling in the speakers by the time I left. For being cultural outsiders, Covenant students usually had their fingers on the pulse of culture at large and were often slightly ahead of the curve. It was the curse of a sober, self-conscious hipsterdom combined with a rigorous, engaged theology.

Covenant Haiku

Branches tap against
the window glazed with rain.
I listen and nap.

A rusty shovel
cutting frozen forest floor,
an opossum's grave.

A mourning dove sings
as I walk towards breakfast.
Melancholy joy.

It is a dreadful
thing to fall into the hands
of the living God.

Sitton's Cave

Turning off my light I began to see
shapes in the darkness
before my open, blind eyes.
There in the cave, miles from light,
human faces loomed false, shifting.
Flicking my headlamp back on,
my pupils retracted suddenly,
and there was only mud,
pillars of rock, a gravel stream-bed,
and my own human breath
coming out in clouds.

Homesters and Hip-schoolers

Everyone dresses the same,
each one as different as the next.
Alone together on a mountaintop,
ironic and awkwardly original,
living with baseball players
and ballroom dancers. Each week
is a new band for listening
and the same old board game
comforting as a mother's kiss.
Such a collision of similar differences,
such a strange flavor of art
in the collision of air, warm and cool,
spiraling out like a storm
blowing the leaves off trees,
orange and brown, each one
uniquely the same.
We feast on moral hedonism.
We dance in the most appropriate,
extravagant imitation of the forefront fad.
All these leggings and jeggings
and mom-jeans on men
who stay up late baking brownies
and then walk to class through the wind
their rolling suitcases thundering quietly
their trench-coats melding with the clouds.

III. Christianity

Christianity

Christianity is a pro-poetry religion. The English word "poem" is originally derived from the Greek word "poeien" which means "to create." Equally, the word "poet" at its root means "creator." Thus, if God is the great Creator, he is also the great Poet, and all of creation is his poem, spoken into existence.

And what is more, he has made us humans in his divine image, as little poets, and given us the task of naming all that has been created. We participate in the making of the world with our words.

Loving poetry is a biblical stance. The creation story in the beginning of the Book of Genesis is a Hebrew poem, loaded down with parallelism. And that is no fluke. By some accounts, nearly seventy-five percent of the Old Testament is poetry. Clearly God has a bias towards good words well chosen, and so it should come as no surprise when Jesus is called "The Word made flesh."

Now, I have a great deal of affection for religion, Christianity in particular, and it is an affection that I know not everyone shares. There are a variety of reasons for folks to dislike religion: it's boring; it's the opiate of the masses; it's pre-modern mumbo jumbo; it's for the weak and cowardly; and it's judgmental and violent. There are personal reasons too. Many people have been hurt by family members or friends wielding religion like a club.

I oppose this sort of religion. I'm not into religion that claims dancing is from the devil. I'm not into fundamentalism in its many forms, but I do think religion is fundamental for human beings.

We don't stop worshipping when we don't have a specific religion, we just build different gods. The cult of celebrity is one particularly shallow option. The shrine of ego and personal success is extremely common too. Often, folks look to the almighty throne of technology to provide true salvation outside of themselves. And it would make sense to worship technology. Technology claims to solve our problems. I am speaking of technology, not just in terms of any one machine or one tool, but of the cultural force of technology that demands efficiency, productivity, and speed from its followers in the name of progress. It is worth pointing out that efficiency, productivity, and speed are very different values from kindness, freedom, and love.

There are many other modern gods as well. Consumerism, capitalism, and communism all have their own strategies for salvation, and each common addiction is a demon unto itself. We are possessed by alcohol, painkillers, pornography, and hoarding. We destroy our own lives against our wills. We are religious people who have lost our religious vocabulary. We feed ourselves to other powers, and delude ourselves into thinking it is not worship.

So instead, I would argue that we should worship the god Yahweh, the divine poet of creation, the liberator of slaves, the righteous one, who took on flesh as Jesus Christ, a god above history within history, who preached and practiced non-violence, who went about healing people and doing good, who died on the cross, who rose from the grave, who ascended into heaven, whose kingdom is coming on earth, whose Spirit moves among us as a rushing wind, who settles on us as a tongue of fire, who moves us still. It may seem cliché, but I believe in this God of grace revealed in Jesus Christ. And I believe this God likes poems.

The Locust and the Cactus Flower

Stone-worn feet have walked before
with blood and sweat and desert faith
till stumbling, jumbled bones be more.

So stark, sharp ribs which honor for
the warm soul's companion wraith
yet stone-worn feet have walked before

with callused humble hands, not poor
though owning nothing, hopeful slaves
till stumbling, jumbled bones be more.

Such painful grace to love a whore
a pure, odd monk must thus behave
yet stone-worn feet have walked before

the priestly prophet through death's door
three days and forty nights the grave
till stumbling, jumbled bones be more.

Ascetic logic, holy gore:
that tortured flesh our souls should save
yet stone-worn feet have walked before
till stumbling, jumbled bones be more.

Lent

The Beloved is driven out
cast into the wilderness.
That same Spirit, descending dove,
seizes the Son by the shoulders.
shakes him, shoves, drives
him as if with a whip, as if
he was cattle. What Love is this?
Is this the way of the Lord?
A voice cries out in the wilderness,
"The easy way is not quick.
The hard route is the sure route.
Repent and believe."
Christ goes out to meet Satan.
Christ cradles the venom of this world.
striking us an odd and monkish man,
ruddy and full-fleshed, callused,
wind-leathered, sunburnt, close to tears.
The very maker of hills sits in silence.
He who crafted the fractal fracturing of rock,
who holds the hardness of stone in place,
is now the hungry one, empty and weak.
This is the way of the Lord
for Love is a terrible thing,
full of courage.

Of Nazareth

Jesus walks in pumped-up kicks,
low impact for his weak knees,
shape-up shoes for tight glutes.
Soft shoulders carry the cross,
or not.
      Instead to marry
a bubbly Bible-college beauty
and raise paunchy, pale babies.
Fluorescent-tube middle-management.
Bible study coffee for breakfast.
Why resurrect for more?

Youth Pastor

This parking-lot poem is directed
towards the youth pastor with a soul patch,
proudly Texan, or at the very least,
openly suburban. Son of sprawl, how can you
draw these rich children to Christ,
that bruised Middle-Eastern man
making unreasonable requests,
smelling of sawdust, drinking wine?
How can you place that NRA sticker
above the Jesus fish on your
gargantuan Chevy Tahoe?
When the trembling Christ told Peter
to put down his bloody sword
and reached out to heal his enemy,
were you not disarmed too?
I can't help but imagine you
organizing a Superbowl party
and calling it "fellowship"
complete with the chemical aftertaste
of blue-ranch dusted Doritos.
Please shave your soul patch.
Please find your soul.

Kenosis

After the schism, the end
of a long estrangement,
the monks withdrew into the desert,
hiding in caves from the noonday heat.
They chanted the old songs
and starved themselves, little by little.
They kept small gardens, only
an onion or three.
They ate onions like apples,
their breath rising to God.

The Holy Family

They are refugees, gypsies, the holy family
full of fear and promise, speaking
in some strange tongue.
They camp in the lee of garden hedges, whispering,
rising early to avoid the automated lawn sprinkler.
The world is green and empty. There is nothing to eat.

They have wandered from cul-de-sac to cul-de-sac
refilling their water skins from garden hoses.
One morning they ran from the disgruntled charge
of an obese man on a lawn tractor, thinking
him some beast.
They did not know that he was incredibly kind
and only intended to say hello.

The Future is Fast Approaching

The future is fast approaching,
a whirling salvo of dates and minutes,
alarms and chimes and bells tolling
(for whom?). The calendar is blank.
The schedule and to-do list are desolate
like the moon, barren
as Elizabeth, the cousin of Mary.
Which is to say, they will
not remain barren forever.
Prepare the way of the Lord.
Make the crooked paths straight.
The calendar shall fill with events:
choir practice for the voice in the wilderness,
meetings with the bee-keeping association,
a doctor's appointment for viper anti-venom.
The future is a revelation
unrolling like a scroll.
It tastes like honey on the tongue
but turns bitter in the stomach.
The future rides a white horse
and death follows behind
carrying a cross, placing it
as an invisible mark on your calendar,
at a given hour, you shall meet,
you and death together.

The Prophet Samuel

He is the young priest clad in linen,
with his mother printing his initials
in his holy underwear. Each year
his mother brings him new clothes,
new clothes for the sacrificial child
who was given to the temple
to bring new life to his family:
three sons of blessing
two daughters of grace,
they who took the place
of the firstborn son.
Does he give his birthright willingly?
He is the priest-child
in the presence of the Lord.

The Manger Star

The manger star over Bethlehem
kept the innkeeper up and
he swore under his breath
as he closed his shutters.
"All this fuss for a census.
Parades of pregnant women
wandering into town, and
the night lit up like the day.
When can a man get some rest?"
And the shepherds blundered by.

Winepress

The winepress is full of blood
and feet of the workers stamp it down.
The harvest fire is burning the chaff
whipped from the good wheat,
threshed in the heat of the day.

Let us put on our camel hair
and follow the plague of locusts
in their wide path, let us
reach our hand into the hives of bees
pulling the honeycomb out,
thankful for abundance, that
bees make more than they need,
that there is enough.

Lord save us
from the thoughtless pledge
made under the spell of wine
to the fickle, jealous, and vain.
Keep our necks from the
executioner's block, the ignominy
of a silver platter, a trophy
for the wicked, and this body
a headless corpse.

Seven Days

There at the edge of all darkness
where the sharp blade of light
was forged, white-hot, and
plunged into the water of time.

There where the yellow sun said, "Yes."
And the gentle moon said, "Also."
And the stars were silent
as they always are:
smiling like wise fools.

There where the sky reaches down
to touch the ocean, and yet
never succeeds.

There where the great pressure of stone
rises from the ocean still molten
to turn its rocky face to the sky.

There where the swamp grass grows,
the soil soaked to mud, smooth and slick,
footfalls sinking down and sucking loose,
where water rushes to fill the former hole
and plumes of floating dirt cloud up around
each step masking the movements of tadpoles,
frogs, fish. Living things love the warm slime:
groping, growing, chewing, sprouting,
bulbous, blundering, abundant life.

There where the image of God is drawn in dust,
rhyming man with woman.

There where the exhale ends
and active men then rest their hands,
mothers cease the stirring of pots
for the fire gathers the family in;
everything as it should be
soot in the chimney, dust on the rug,
spilled chili still staining the counter.
Let the people come, flushed with creation,
breathing God's breath, to rest.

Autumn Evening

The wind goes where it will.
The wind blows cool through the window
scattering the papers on the desk.
A fresh cup of tea is still steaming
on the corner of the bedside table.
There is an icon of Christ,
gaunt and priestly, on the wall.
His hand is raised in blessing.

Panta Rhei

Who is this God? Constant in flux,
turning rivers to blood and blood to wine
so all the drunks can drink and drown in grace,
always allowing. Gives and gives again always
the water and the blood flowing from his side
or turning the blood we spilled into water
that cries out to heaven, rising
above the highest mountains, cleansing
the earth with its own violence, bloodwaters rising,
always turning, repenting, transforming, always
the two by two, the losers, the remnant,
the impossible hope. The water is wine.
The wine is blood. The blood is water.
The blood is an ever-flowing stream
between two trees. And rocks bring forth
water pouring out and giving again
like the stone the builders rejected,
even when struck it still pours forth
new wine, new wine-skins, new life.
The river is blood as if to say
our living will only bring us death
We must die with God to live.
Baptized in blood, washed in wine,
drunk on water, we turn. We are turned.

Surrexit Rex

Who is this coming king? This already-not-yet regent,
humble, hard, and kind, Lord beyond death,
broken body bursting with life, transfigured
with light, the torture wounds still open
on his resurrected hands? What is
this force of divinity, barely contained,
pulsing in each eternal cell?
No wall, no grave, no tomb,
no stone, no chain, no sword,
could keep the king restrained.
He goes where he wills,
locked rooms and desert roads.
Grave-robber, gardener,
gathering his people to him.
The kingdom of God is near.

IV. Ethiopia

Ethiopia

Ethiopia is a mountain fortress of a country, a bastion of ancient Christianity surrounded on all sides by Islam. Monasteries dot the hillsides and perch precariously on cliffs. Inside them, young novices study the Bible in an archaic language called Ge'ez. Analogous to Sanskrit or Latin, Ge'ez is the language that evolved into modern Amharic but is now used only in liturgies and old books. The novices learn by rote, preserving rather than innovating. They wander the countryside, asking for alms to learn humility.

Ethiopian church buildings resemble Jewish temples more than European cathedrals. The people worship outside the buildings looking in on the holy place under the dome. The holy of holies is hidden from sight. But the similarities to a Jewish temple end there, for Ethiopian churches are covered in icons and murals depicting the heroes of the faith for those who can't read. St. George in particular, with the red-brown skin and curly hair of an Ethiopian, is almost always shown driving his lance into the throat of a dragon. St. George is said to have appeared at the Battle of Adwa and led the Ethiopian forces to rout the Italians, so he holds a special place in Ethiopian hearts for helping fend off colonial aggressors. After watching the priests offer prayers and after offering their own, the worshippers give alms to the beggars at the gate of the church and go home to eat mounds of spicy sauces on a spongy sour-dough flatbread called *injira*.

My parents lived on a Scandinavian seminary in Addis Ababa, an oasis of green in that great grey and brown city. Future Ethiopian pastors studied theology or held prayer meetings on the lawns while Finnish professors made sure that there was enough time to take a sauna every Friday evening. Outside the walls of the seminary, the traffic lurched through the streets. Shepherds drove their goats towards the city abattoir, clogging the intersections with stubborn bleating. Eucalyptus smoke from kitchen fires filled the sky. Even the tourists, walking by the oldest known hominid bones in the world, or stopping to ponder Haile Selassie's small sea-green bathtub, could not escape the smell of burning eucalyptus branches.

There was much to see and much to write.

Ethiopia and Its Airlines

Pesto chicken pasta
and straight black coffee at midnight.
I sit up awake with three chairs to myself.
1 am, 2 am, 3 am.
The cabin goes blue in the sleep light
as we cross the Saharan night sky.
The book of Hebrews and half of a gangster movie,
I stumble out to the 6 am sunrise
in Addis Ababa, a smoky city.
My parents are smiling.

Mekane Yesus Seminary

My parents live beside a river brown
as mud and red as clay. It rises in
the rains to catch the sleepers in their beds.
Just once, before, it came to flood and rot
the house in which they live. So now they know
and do not wait for doom to come at night.
A dam was built, a mound of dirt around
their home, their garden flowers, birds, and porch.
The very clay that stains the stream now stands
on guard against it. Across the creek
dead eucalyptus snags still hold their roots,
their branches out like bones against the sky
to host a jury of vultures
presiding over decay
but on this bank we have another Lord,
the God of finch and feast and birdsong joy.
We sip some tea and rest our feet inside,
all glad for rain that makes the garden grow.

Finding the Treadwells

After my deep, black jetlag nap
we wander this neighborhood,
mother and son amongst
diesel fumes and dust clouds.
You can taste each eye irritant
bitter on your tongue.
Almost lost in mud-flow alleys
we turn with the wide-paved ring-road
happening upon where we wish to be:
a friend's concrete home on a dirt street.

Later, we walked home as dogs fought
and the blue-grey sky opened up
for its afternoon rain-storm.

On the Road to Lake Langano

In Ethiopia, the peasant walks
from home to field and back again,
his plow is heavy on his shoulder bone:
two large poles he lashed together
one long, one shorter with a metal tip.
He yokes his long-faced donkey
and pushes down on the giant lever
turning the black volcanic soil once more.
Does he ever rest beneath the acacia thorns
and drink a tiny cup of bitter coffee?
These are rocky open plains,
a land with donkeys toting bales of straw
each load three times their height:
little tottering siege towers of hay
climbing expansive hills in arid highlands.
All is under sun. All is dust and thorn.
And still he brings
bright wheat from good dark dirt.

Mount Mowgli

We climb through the scrub brush,
tiny pine needles fall down our shirts,
pricking the skin on our necks.
And then, as we reach the summit
accompanied by the dinosaur chirrup
of thick-billed ravens, soaring and rolling,
we look down on the gray city:
the tan-yellow apartment buildings,
the Orthodox churches tucked in
on arched cobblestone streets,
the dust, the pollution, the trash,
the beggars and the mentally ill
who talk to walls with great earnestness,
who dance in spirals with little hand mirrors
held out in front of their ecstatic faces,
who shuffle in chains, begging
for money in grocery store parking lots.

The air is thin on the mountaintop.
This the tallest mountain in a ring
of rounded peaks and knolls that jut up
around the horizon of the city, the capital.

We began our walk where Emperor Menelik
once had his hunting palace
high up in his protected forest,
where kings were crowned and
rode down through the shade

of ancient junipers
to rule their African empire.

Later, these proud people killed.
their own emperor for his corruption,
but instead of bringing peace,
they taught themselves terror and hunger
in a schizophrenic world dictated
by two cold northern empires.
They still hold scars
from the torture and mistrust of that time,
but continue to live, growing barley,
harvesting by hand on steep hills.

Even in the warmth of the bright, close sun
we feel the wind blow cold and thin.
We turn back from the mountaintop.

Balé Mountains

Islamic men ride by in the mountain pass,
checkered scarves over gaunt cheeks
and red-brown Ethiopian skin.
Their horses are short and sure-footed,
as shaggy as their goat-skin riding blankets.
They weave through the heather
and drop down into the dark juniper forests
where their families wait for them,
children tending the goats,
wives watching the barley turn gold.

We follow the ridge-line, covered in heather,
tracing deep-cut paths set in turf and stone
before entering the shadows of the forest too.
We are glad to find the cabin
with one kerosene lamp lit in its window.
The whole dark room smells of kerosene:
the old noble tea-pot, black on its edges,
the creaking, worn wooden benches,
a place for the foot-sore and short of breath.
It is one warm shadow of a room,
dark as coal or soot, smelling of kerosene.

May God bless those Islamic men.
May He fill their houses with bread.
May He give them rest.

V. Togo

Togo

Togo is a tiny country along the coast of West Africa. It was formerly part of the larger African kingdom of Dahomey before the region was split between the French and the Germans in the colonial scramble for Africa. After World War I and Germany's defeat, the German colony was split again between the victors: Britain and France. Modern-day Togo was allotted to France, and modern-day Ghana was awarded to Britain. Language groups, political affiliations, and economic ties were ignored, and new lines were drawn. Colonization has a long history of such foolishness, or what is worse, carefully calculated disempowerment.

I was in Togo to complete a research internship on church-based, savings-led micro-finance. After spending a few days in Lomé, a capital city crammed full of Chinese motorcycles and French architecture, I traveled to Kpalimé, a beautiful little town at the foot of the Volta hills. While Lomé offered wide sand beaches and bustling boulevards, I found I preferred the winding jungle roads and hidden waterfalls of Kpalimé.

We spent a great deal of time at churches as part of our research, and Togolese church services are loud. The sound-system was usually cranked all the way up, largely so the lead singer could be heard over the teenage boy on the snare drum, seemingly set on destroying the skin of the drum through the sheer insistency of his rhythm. Without fail, the old women of the church, regal in their elaborate dresses and head wraps, would get up to shuffle and dance around the front of the church. The rhythm and repetition was an invitation to participate, to achieve a sort of ecstasy that was denied people working long days in the markets or the manioc fields. Worship was an occasion to sweat.

Togo felt like a particularly productive time for me as a poet. Perhaps it was because I had just taken a poetry class at Covenant the semester before, and so my control of iambs, anapests, and trochees was fluid and fit. Perhaps it was because I was traveling and the new experiences were grist for the poetic mill. Perhaps it was because I was working as a researcher, and so most of my job was just to pay attention to things and write them down, a practice which lends itself well to the discipline of poetry. For whatever reason, I wanted to write, I felt able to write, and there was plenty to write about. These are some of those poems.

Addis to Lomé

I spent six hours
wedged into the armpit
of an overflowing Togolese diplomat,
bright in his traditional garb
as he hunched over his iPad,
refusing to raise his tray table
for take-off and landing.

Lomé — Les Jeunes Hommes

The young they swell the town with heat and life.
The roads are full of motorcycle men.
Coffee for breakfast, or nothing at all
and then another day of errands to run
on broad and sandy streets by palm
and mango trees, each guardian of life
with shade to share for each to each:
the thin mechanic and the carpenter,
the ice-cream salesman pedaling slow
and sounding his clown horn by hand.
They each put on their dress sandals,
their slacks and sunglasses, clean above the clay
and step out into the street
to make the city move and live again,
brightly clothed and sweating in the sunshine.

Dirt Makes Food Makes Dirt

We have nothing to do but dance
in the flatland, dustland,
dirtland, mudland, maize growing,
corn kernels shaking inside a gourd
or other vessels: spoons and cups
brimming over with palm wine;
nothing to do but dance and drum:
go to church and dance,
watch TV and dance,
bass drum, snare drum, cowbell, djembe,
harvest the root and dance,
harvest the beans and dance,
yam dance, demon dance, freedom dance,
raise your children to dance,
even toddlers nod their heads
and shake their hips as they
stumble by the music store
which shares its wares for free
with all who live nearby:
the Bible salesmen next door,
napping as the bass beat
shakes his walls and rattles his shelves,
the hairdresser with a blue felt carpet
barefoot, coiling braids, humming along,
the child of the street vendor
tossing marbles at lines in the dirt,
nothing to do but dance:
the twist of the knee and

the single shoulder twitch,
a moment of forgetfulness
to remember where you are
and what you are and that
your body has bones and elbows,
biceps, triceps, and a belly button,
thick skin on the bottom of your feet
ground brown as the dust.
This day will only come once
and tomorrow will be the same
with nothing to do but dance.

Noonday

Rain-clouds are building on the horizon
but here the sun shines straight down
so that each passerby's forehead
is glistening with beads of sweat:

The woman with the giant basin on her head
brimming with un-shelled peanuts
adjusting her wrap as she walks
to cinch the baby to her back

or the friendly man without his senses
grimacing as he talks, showing brown teeth.
He wears a cowboy hat, but no shoes.
He wants to show you a picture
of himself in 1982. There are
two people in the picture, a young
black man and a white boy
He points himself out.
What has happened since 1982?
that now he is singing, loud and slurring,
sweating in the noonday sun,
"Mother Mary comes to me. Lerrit be."
But still his voice is strong
wishing blessings upon strangers.

He is not the man in the yellow shirt
whose voice is husky with smoke,
Not the man who tells you things

you barely understand and
things you wish you didn't.
For that man stands just down the street
in his front yard burning trash,
around him lies 3,000 empty tin cans.
His yellow eyes are drunk and vacant.
His mother was a whore.
His father is blind.
His sister spends everything
on alcohol and cigarettes.
The sun is hot.
His mother was a whore.
The sun is hot.
His father is blind.
Do you understand?

Two-hundred kindergartners march by
in tiny grey uniforms. Their
teachers keep the rhythm with shakers
and lead them in their song.
Fifty children per teacher. The little ones,
they swing their arms and sing and stomp
and laugh and cry and tumble
 to the ground, not too far away,
and run to catch their friends again.

This afternoon the rain will pour
all at once and soak the air
so that the night can come all cool and calm
with stars between the clouds.

A Haiku Understanding of Complexity

Who finished the rum
bottle once full of candy
peanuts? Tell me now.

The little boy is
running naked in the rain.
Who is he fighting?

Each path is a stream
from the afternoon rain now
the sunset ripples

The African man,
sleeping on the dining room
table, is snoring.

Auriel, Gabriel, and Raphael

Whispering tall grass,
the horizon is blue dark,
a wall of grey mist.

The sky is growling
at the lone baobab tree.
I turn back for home.

Each saw-grass blade leans
out into the path, heavy
with water droplets.

The path is worn down
hard-scabble, turtle-shell dirt,
tiny rivers in sand.

Wetland water flows
clear under this walkway plank.
A fish darts from view.

Five Haiku and an Utterance, From a Co-Worker En Route to Dinner Pertaining to Intercultural Research

1.

Sitting down to lunch
as a lizard watches us
one unblinking eye

2.

and in Africa
Frenchmen still sit at cafes
drinking beer instead

3.

Underneath the trees,
the world is fresh and cool and good
with fruit on the ground.

4.

Thank you, dearest monks
for making green mango jam,
holy, delicious.

5.

The evangelist
is sweating in the aisle
dancing to the drums.

"I should show it to you.
I have this calendar,
full of things that...
probably won't happen"

Fodder for Poems

-Discussing the military-industrial-complex and the apocalypse on dirt roads while walking to buy paper supplies.

-Trying to explain elves, dwarves, and goblins to someone who has never heard of them, someone who would explain demon possession in terms of what happens next door.

-A 30yr old African pastor who feels abandoned by Baptist missionaries from Michigan. They left when he was 13. He named his son after their son, his best friend. He thinks it is his destiny to meet Americans.

-Giving a "gift" to the caretaker of a plundered palace to pace the empty rooms.

-The sandy center aisle of a mango grove cathedral. A baobab rises up like a steeple.

- Little boys running down rocky roads pretending to be airplanes. These three foot pariahs give us flowers and ask for money, stopping just short of rifling their hands through our pockets.

-Two boys running along, smacking motorcycle tires with the flat of their machetes to keep the battered things rolling.

-A three year old picking up pebbles to drop in a cup, and then taking out them out again.

-A 23 year old UN peacekeeper who has left the army to follow Jesus. We talk about Lil Wayne in our second languages.

-A farmer with yellow flowers all around his 3 circular cottages. One cottage is full of tiny drums which the neighborhood kids pound furiously whenever they get a chance.

-Chickens taking dust baths. Chickens sprawled out in the sun. Chickens fornicating in the tall grass. Chickens cooked in peanut sauce.

-Black granite on a German grave (1871-1904).

-The thin line of ants hissing in the jungle.

-A worm the size of a small snake, wriggling on the jungle mountain highway in the rain.

A Rider on a Pale Horse

This is a retelling of a dream
 recounted to me. It was told
in a dark restaurant as the entire world
stormed and thundered outside
and candles flickered on our concrete table.

"When I was young I dreamed.
In my dream
I found myself lost, alone,
standing on an open plain
beneath the night sky when
the moon and the stars
came crashing down to earth.
I did not know what was happening;
I did not know the end of the world
for I was young then.
The moon and stars came crashing down
and there was a great darkness
and from that great darkness
suddenly an immense flame.
I was lost, alone,
I did not know what was happening,
and I saw angels
tossing bodies into the flames:
my friends, my cousins, my brothers,
those who were close to me,
and I asked, 'Why?
Why is this happening?'

For I was young

and did not know the end of the world.

I was alone in great darkness

the moon and stars had fallen.

When I awoke

I became a quiet child

I told no-one of my dream

but considered what I had seen

and I thought to myself,

'I will enjoy my youth,

I will take my pleasure

then in my old age

I will become a Christian.'

For I was young

and did not know the end of the world.

I did not know."

Kloto

Some German ghosts still haunt the hills all dark
and silent in their giant empty windows.
They sit and watch the valley: bright and green,
medieval with the town's cathedral spire,
the cross above the trees and all around
are trees, leaves arching over like a cave
the world is bending, always hiding in
the curve behind the tree or past the bush.
The pillars of the German home remain
but they are chipped and cracked and crumbled down
all scrawled with names, each claiming love,
the devil, Christ, some mystery made flesh,
and yet the roof still keeps the rafters dry
despite the rains that come each year
to rot the wood and grow the trees to rot
again. The tin is slowly rusting too.

Beneath them all
a man is standing still,
at the tip of a curve in the path
he looks out on the valley, his sling
and stone in hand to kill a bird. Perhaps
he knows that death is often sudden like
the moto-taxi speeding, engine off
to barrel down each silent mountain curve
but death is also sickly sweet and rotting,
the force of life when turned upon itself,
the many mangoes scattered on the roadside.

And still the people pray and clear some land
to plant and harvest pineapple. And come
when it will come, for each and everyone,
they are buried in a cemetery
with bathroom tiles decorating their tombstones.

Le Vautour et Le Chauve-Souris

A brooding hunch of vultures
bald and burnt in the late afternoon
watching over the old tin roof
of the three-room slaughterhouse,
the subtle stench, the dark red floor
shining the same shade as a dying sunset.

Dusk rises from the earth.
Bats are flying south
along the edge of the mountains,
a great host of bats,
talon and fur and pointed ears
spread thin across the sky
like the remaining wisps of rainclouds.
The world is obscurity and darkness.

And in the coming blackness
a red moon rises, casting faint shadows.
The grass is whispering rumors to the palm trees.

Choir Practice with Bystanders

He gimp limp swing steps, elegant lurching,
through the open night door
dark skin bright shining in the moonlight
a single staff crutch clutched tight.
Each step is ponderously placed
for a moment solid and still before
the pole vault arching fall step
back to balance and harmony.
Half step, whole step, church steps
African choir singing to full moon shadows.
He paces the plaza, pausing to listen,
asks for the absent pastor, pivots in place,
and passes into the night shadows,
the choir still swaying to a back track.

Sunday Sunrise: Kpalimé: July 28 2013

Early in the morning I walk to church,
a sweet cup of tea still warm in my stomach.
The gray clouds are sitting low in the sky,
rubbing their bellies on the tops of the trees.
Everyone outside in the morning dusk
is clad in colors not yet bright with the day,
but shining all the same in anticipation.
A girl runs by in high heels, late for church,
somehow upright despite each stumbling stone
and rounded rock sticking up from the sandy streets.
The doors of the cathedral are wide open.
The dark-wood pews are creaking with prayer.
It is dim in the vaulted room of the church,
formless except for the bright-white habits of nuns,
void and silent but for the many murmured prayers.

The sun is rising to fill each vivid-blue pane
of stained glass, glowing from the east.
Then trumpets speak forth, drums and trumpets
announcing that the new week is good.
And indeed it is very good.
The choir is a single voice walking in step,
speaking out from the center of the church,
What they sing is what I see:
the church is full of light;
the people are risen.

The day before while walking in the fields
I heard the Ramadan call to prayer
faint and far over the rows of maize.
That call is louder in the marketplace
where each pious shopkeeper
sits on the front step of his store
a kettle of water by his feet
rinsing his ears, his eyes, his lips
attempting to undo the evil of that day.
Yet underneath his skin he is a leper,
and remains a leper still.

But we are all lepers here, fools and farmers,
the ragged mass beneath the steeple.
We are all lepers cleansed in dirty river water,
for surely that is the baptism of the church,
a real hope in the mud of troubled waters,
somehow clean amidst our filth flowing on.

And God gathers us in,
like a mother hen brooding over her chicks,
even this morning he has gathered us in love:
his daughters in multi-colored fabric,
his sons with clan scars marking their cheeks,
the young and old of the church,
his unity of diversity, his new creation.

Today is confirmation day
the youth stand up to proclaim their faith.
We stand in solidarity:

One Lord, One Faith, One Baptism.
Solidarity in death.
Solidarity in resurrection.
The people of God
with tired feet and aching backs,
sure of what we cannot see,
bound by love to the one who loves us,
singing forth when we cannot speak.

Now the sun is risen indeed,
and the day has risen to meet it.
I walk home in the dust and noise,
happy to watch my feet on the ground.

We Have Eaten the Last Mango

Two hours through the African evening,
watching the orange sun as it sets,
turning a green forest from blue to black.
Passing on each blind curve
as the fuel light flickers on
we stop to pick up another passenger:
a large woman to crush the skinny man,
mustache and all, who once held the front seat.
The driver toggles his tape player.
The music is from Cote d'Ivoire,
speakers just behind our heads
sending the harmony of drums
out into the gathering darkness
as the singer calls politicians to task.
We know we are approaching the city
as we pass the Chinese mansion:
a white building with a red flag.
And then into the city, dust and darkness
and Christmas lights on Togolese night clubs.
Our music meets theirs in the night air
so everyone can dance in the headlights,
briefly blind but alive.
The driver always forces forward
as though size can make its own space.
But then a man is yelling through the windshield,
potbellied and sweating, plain-clothed
but for the machine-gun on his shoulder.
He gestures in frustration at our driver

who forced his way into a checkpoint,
clogging an already impossible intersection.
Another young man, uniformed,
appears at our window, speaking with authority,
"Everyone must exit the vehicle"
or was it his gun that spoke?
We shook his hand and said, "Bon soir,"
and his smile was bright in the darkness.
We walked for fifty yards by the side of the road
around puddles in the sand
to get back into the same taxi,
searching for someplace safe to spend the night.

VI. Montana

Montana

John Steinbeck once wrote, "I'm in love with Montana. For other states I have admiration, respect, recognition, and even some affection. But with Montana it is love. And it's difficult to analyze love when you're in it." I am also in love with Montana, though my feeling is not the same infatuation as Steinbeck. I have an inherited love for Montana, for it is the home of my mother, a woman who critiques the form of Olympic skiers from her living room in East Africa.

Montana rises from the brutal, barren plains in the east to the alpine meadows and the perpetual snow fields of the mountains in the west. Along the way you must navigate the labyrinthian, crumbling hills of the badlands and the thick pine forests that darken the feet of the mountains.

My mother grew up in the Northwestern corner of Montana, in the Flathead Valley just south of Glacier National Park. My siblings and I inherited a pride in being mountain people, along with a certain disdain for those poor souls who found themselves living on the plains. For us, the plains were simply an obstacle on the way to the mountains. Though in all fairness, the flatlands of Montana are gorgeous; they just aren't the mountains.

We spent our childhood summers in those mountains. We would hike up to glacial lakes and jump in out of pure stubbornness, even though the emerald green water was cold enough to drive all the air out of our lungs. We learnt to hike long distances, to glissade down summer snow fields, to pick tufts of mountain goat hair out of the scrubby alpine trees of the high meadows. We didn't understand that we were in a sort of paradise. Or maybe we did, when we sat on the bumper of our grandpa's Cadillac and drank a cold root beer, knocking the trail dust off our boots, redirecting our focus from the mountain passes of the day to the dinner of spare ribs and strawberry-rhubarb pie that would greet us down in the valley.

I travelled back to Montana in college, though not to spend time in the high valleys and mountain passes. Instead, I spent a few summers working for one of my parents' old friends who ran a ranch in central Montana, not too far from a town called Roundup. The land there was just beginning to roll into low hills. Ponderosa pine trees grew in shallow soil, right next to the sand-stone bedrock. If you traveled another half an hour east, the plains started to open up, but the ranch was hidden in a maze of low hills and valleys. They are technically called the Bull Mountains on a map, the reason being that bison bulls used to weather the winters in the hills to avoid the violent winds on the plains. I would ride around the ranch, imagining those huge, hairy animals wandering from ridge-line to ridge-line, dropping down to the creek side periodically for water, sleeping under the over-hanging sandstone outcroppings.

The work on the ranch was varied and strenuous. One constant task was building and repairing barbed wire fence. We pulled wires taut and straight, spliced new wire to patch holes, and replaced rotten posts. Even with elk-skin gloves, our arms and hands were often scrawled over with tears and cuts from barbed wire by the end of a day's work.

When it was cold, I learnt to cut metal with a blow-torch and weld it back together in a shower of sparks. When other work wasn't pressing, I would sharpen a shovel on the bench grinder and ride through the pastures chopping thistles. Often times I found myself on an ATV, chasing an escaped bull, the both of us getting angrier by the second. Other times I found myself riding a horse to keep a large group of cattle moving in the right direction towards the next pasture.

My first horse was a chestnut named Buck, but we never figured out how to get along. He kept on trying to live up to his name, so I moved on to a one-eyed red horse with no name. She would start to drift diagonally if you didn't pay attention, and you had to let her have her head every once in a while so she could check her blind spot. We got along pretty well. I wanted to name her Rooster, but my boss didn't think that made much sense.

Ranching these days involves very few people and a whole armada of machines. We drove pick-ups, ATV's, skid-steers, tractors, and combines. The skid-steers had an array of hydraulic attachments that could loudly and quickly kill you, or pound down fence-posts, or roll up a half-mile of barbed wire. It was of great importance that you didn't put your hand in the wrong place at the wrong time. Machines are not kind to human bodies.

I didn't have buckets of energy to pour out on poetry after spending ten hours clearing fence-line with a chainsaw, but I did write a few poems. Here they are.

Yagu

He is a solid block of cowflesh,
this opaque hunk of tar-black hide
and stubborn obsidian eyes,
who stumps around the meadows
beleaguered by biting flies that
swarm his broad shoulders and hinds.
The bull is a tank or a battering ram,
a sledgehammer barely conscious,
flinging great gobs of spit on his back
in a futile fight against the flies.
He bellows his disapproval
with flies, with fences, with other bulls,
lusting all alone in his pasture.
This bull is miserable.
This bull deserves it.

Skid-steer

The skid-steer was down in the gully,
its pneumatic hammer poised to pound
down fence-posts into the rocky soil when
the tank tread rolled a fallen log
and out came the snake, rattling
as it went, coiling up and rattling,
sounding its death-warning
then disappearing under another log,
furious as murder to be so disturbed.
I went to find a shovel
in order to sever its venomous head,
but when I returned my boss
had already crushed its writhing body
under the heavy treads of the skid-steer.
We all looked on in horrible fascination,
still fearing the snake's last moments of life,
yet the skid-steer, that grumbling machine,
seemed indifferent
as if life and death were no concern.

Up the Valley

The black cows seem like shadows
in the valley and silhouettes
on the ridges, I would think them
bovine illusions were it not
for the swarms of flies that
harass the twitching, bellowing, itching
heifers, their long black eyelashes
over pure black eyes, their heads
dropped down to crop
at the grass, eating grass
mostly because it's there. No reason really.
Only because they are cows.

Preparations for Moving In

Moving into the new house I found
a dead mouse in the middle of a room,
looking limp on the carpeted floor,
but stiff as a twig and just as light.
He was storing bits of cotton in the stove;
anyone can see. I wonder
what finally brought him to the middle
of that large room and how
did he come to lie there so peaceful,
a small bump of mouse-flesh
with nothing left to do?

Outside, there was a bone in the grass
when I went to mow the lawn.
I had paused the machine to spare the lives
of the little inflated toads
fleeing to the tall grass,
and I saw the bone,
a solitary joint without limb,
bleached white and decaying,
sitting next to a mound of river-stones.
Did not Death stand with me there?
Even as I wiped sweat from my eyes?

Pulp

Nothing but paperbacks stacked
cover to cover, six thousand pages tall
in the largely empty closet.
Picking them up, a back cover
rips off, damp and stuck to the shelf.
The bottom book is moist with fungus.
The other books are dry but
who would want to read them?
Glorifying the cavalry's battles
to steal this land from the Lakota,
all the books by the same formula writer.
Close the closet door. Let them rot.

Late One Evening

Late one evening on the ranch
I left the house to walk the dust
and gravel serving as a road,
away from the bright windows, out
under an abundance of stars.
who, in multitudes, shone just
enough to show my faint shadow
striding out before me.
In the dim and obscure night glow,
I turned left at a crossroads
drawn by the rising moon to the river
which danced the moon twice, rippling
the silver light, the smooth stones grumbling.
And in the autumn chill, I climbed
the iron trellises of the abandoned railroad bridge
to stand suspended in the sky
amongst the stars,
above the water,
dizzy with solitude,
before carefully clambering down in the dark.

Welding Fence Braces

We harness lightning to hold metal in place,
a fierce arc of electricity licking
metal puddles back and forth:
globs of slag spatter and drip and
a fountain of sparks sprays up out
of the blue-white, blinding light
biting and burning into a melted seam.
It is a brilliant and focused heat
leaving layers of liquid metal
running in to fill the cracks.

And when you work welding,
staring through a dark pane,
the kevlar-woven pig-skin gloves
reaching halfway up your forearms
are unable to shield you from
the honey-sweet smell of red-hot iron.
You are not protected from
and the sharp ringing of the hammer
as you knock flakes of brittle slag loose.
The sky is a cold slab of grey
and the iron is glowing orange
and you can feel the heat
baking the wind-worn skin on your face,
skin which hardens and cools like metal.

Fewer Bugles Every Night

Elk hunters mill about their trucks
preparing to go out, just before the evening.
They tighten quivers to their backs
and fetch their bows, testing the strings.
The fat one gets a rifle.

Labor

Stepping out into the frosted morning
we hastily seized each boot with both hands
and drove cold feet into those aching spaces,
hopping up to the truck with
sandwich lunches and water bottles
packed away in stained and torn backpacks.
We pulled our jeans over our boots
with scratched and scarred hands
and hunched our shoulders against the cold,
eagerly awaiting the same sun
we had cursed at noon the day before
when it had taxed our strained wills, so
tired of wrestling barbed wire into place.
The diesel engine finished compressing.
All that remained was to turn the key.

Part-way There

When the truck broke down
on the rutted dirt road of the ranch,
we had a large hill at our backs
and could only push forward,
thanking heaven for the light alloy
of the Mitsubishi mini-truck.
Shifting into neutral we rolled
onwards at the pace of pioneers,
oxcarts digging pathways into the prairies.
We strained up a slight incline,
gravel rolling out from under our boots,
and rumbled across the cattle-guard,
using the gaps to gain purchase.
As the earth tilted ever so slightly
away and out from under us
I stood up on the trailer hitch
of our tiny truck rolling free.
I was proud as a captain
at the helm of his ship
watching the horizon and then
jumping back down again
bending over to focus on the dirt
around my feet, to focus
on pushing the broken truck.

Cows and Trees

Pine trees rise out of rim-rock sandstone
with the black shadows of cows
passing between them, flowing
down to the gully
where the grass is soft and sweet.
By the end of the summer
these trees may catch fire
and burn a white-hot death.
There is a beauty in that.
But what hope have the cows?

VII. Nepal

Nepal

After college, I spent a summer in Kathmandu, teaching English to a gifted and kind group of Nepali students preparing for university. I would teach class for three intensive hours in the morning, and then go looking for lunch nearby. One of the cheapest and most delicious options was a plate of steamed Nepali dumplings called *momo* served with a piercing mustard dip. After *momo* for lunch, I would order a cup of honey-ginger tea, sit in a rooftop cafe, and do my lesson planning for the next day. After a dinner of *palak paneer* with *naan* from one of the many Indian restaurants in the neighborhood, I would go to bed under a mosquito net. I counted myself lucky to be alive.

Kathmandu is a large city crammed into a mountain valley. The exhaust from the tuk-tuks, motorcycles, buses, trucks, and cars settles in the back of your throat after a week or so. At the end of the dry season, there is a steady cloud of dust to accompany the exhaust, and so the air quality suffers even more. The monsoon season is a welcome respite from the dust and heat, but all too often the rains flood the narrow streets, up past the axles of cars, and the flood-waters creep into the doorways of first floor shops. The alleyways and side-streets turn into rushing creeks flowing down to any of the eight rivers that run through the valley. It is inconvenient, to be sure, but in some ways it is quite beautiful to see your street turn into a churning river.

Nepal is culturally and economically tied to India, the giant to the south, and thus Hinduism is a huge cultural force. Little shrines to contorted gods can be found on most street corners, and due to the sacredness of cows in Hinduism, one would have a hard time finding a restaurant that sells beef. Instead, most of the butchers in the city sell "buff," which is water buffalo meat. It's an odd dietary loophole, but I was not complaining. If anything, I may prefer water buffalo meat to beef. Buff *momo* is delectable.

Even with the widespread influence on food, Hinduism does not have a monopoly on the religious landscape. Nepal is the birth place of Prince Siddhartha, who became the Buddha, and so there is no lack of Buddhist temples, monasteries, and *stupas*. Buddhist monks and Buddhist nuns are plentiful in Kathmandu. Both shave their heads and wear billowing saffron-red robes, so it can be hard to tell them apart if one is not paying close attention. I have only my personal observations to rely on, but it seems monks love buff *momo* too.

In the City

The city has many things:
the cow with a shattered horn,
the stray dog asleep on the road,
the mischievous smile of a monk,
a large plate of rice.

Kathmandu

And just like that, the rains come down
all at once, the summer monsoon
to drive down the dust to the muddy ground.
Puddles on the pavement, rivers in the street,
a rising flood to carry all the refuse,
the cigarette butts and watermelon rinds
floating down the ditches into the poisoned,
swelling river. And the people still walk
just as they did in the dust and heat,
umbrellas up to shield off the rain.
They go about their business the same.
Yesterday, the sun as bright as a headache,
today, the cool, gray rain falling softly.
And the conductors on the public buses
still hang, half out of their sliding doors,
clutching grimy stacks of small bills,
yelling out all twelve stops in one
unbroken breath, as if it were one word.
Some conductors no older than fourteen,
squinting their eyes against the falling rain,
pounding the sides of their vans
in basic drum-speak: Go. Stop.
It is good that the monsoon comes,
that the crops grow, that the dust settles,
And just like that, the city washes clean.

Stupa

Tourists in tight-fitting shorts sit
earnestly meditating next to monks
who also sit red-cloaked, row on row
chanting from memory in a deep hum.
The monks' eyes are open, peering around,
fashionable sunglasses perched on their shaved heads,
watching the less earnest tourists watching them.
This is one route to enlightenment.
Prosperous monks desire nothing.

Stupa Haiku

Small baby Buddha
born in Nepal, drinking milk.
What do you desire?

Koheleth

Pilgrims walk clockwise around the stupa,
spinning wheels and burning prayer scrolls.
They disturb the crowds of pigeons,
startled into the air by the shuffling feet
cracked, calloused, and accustomed to walking.

And there is the old woman, brown and dark,
screaming in what must surely be anger,
frantically reaching out to spin
a large, brass, ornate wheel, like a giant bell,
embossed with scenes from the life of Buddha.
Why is she screaming? Why does she spin the wheel?

There are special prayer wheels set apart,
housed like millstones in special rooms
and the wheel never stops spinning
all through the night, all through the day,
the great wheel turns and turns with prayer
just as the world continues to turn
just as the sun rises and the sun sets
before returning to where it began.
There is no end to these things
and even pleasure grows tiresome.

Long ago, this is what the teacher found:
meaningless, meaningless, everything is meaningless
vanity of vanities, dust and smoke,
everything is but a feeding on the wind.

11:30 pm

Awoken from an uneasy dream,
I hear a faint rustling on the carpet floor
and jump out of bed to switch on the light.
There in my doorway, each standing a half-inch tall
are two squat-legged cockroaches conspiring,
pausing on my welcome mat as though
to consider the risk of entering the room.
What do they hope to find?
I kill one with a flip-flop
while the other scuttles away,
disappearing under a locked door.

After the Monsoon Rain

I took an old bicycle out
onto the streets of Kathmandu,
precariously dodging potholes and
smiling at the kind shop-owner
who stitched ornate saris
to feed her only daughter.
And she laughed at me on my bicycle
bouncing down the uneven alleyway
playing the holy fool on a tightrope
with no particular destination in mind.

Badi Village

It was not the first time
the pastor had visited the brothel,
a powerful man amongst girls.
He barters with the pimps
(some of them parents)
to buy the girls and take them
away with himself.

And the pastor does not touch them.
He is always buying girls
and sending them to school.
The pimps don't know.
The pastor will destroy them.

When the Rains Come

Heavy humid air has settled on the city.
There will be weddings when the rains come.
A dead pigeon, wrapped in newspaper, lies in the gutter.
There will be weddings when the rains come.

Exhaust pours out the tailpipe of a water truck.
There will be weddings when the rains come.
An old monk beats two irreverent boys with his cane.
There will be weddings when the rains come.

A prayer horn drones in the distance.
There will be weddings when the rains come.
A deaf waiter patiently waits for his words to be seen.
There will be weddings when the rains come.

VIII. Airports

Airports

The act of traveling challenges us to see things for the first time again, and we are struck by the elegance, absurdity, and bustle of people's lives. The haggard faces of strangers become luminous and fascinating.

These poems grew out of the slow time between flights, when you have plenty of time to find your airport gate, but not enough to time to leave the airport, not enough time to see the strange city, and not enough time to pass through security again without the risk of missing your flight. So you sit at your airport gate and inspect your fellow passengers. You watch a cross-sample of the human race walking down the airport hallways, and you speculate about their lives, each person an oddity unto themselves.

I become fascinated with people's shoes in airports. There are those who cherish fashion over utility, even to the point of pain. There are those for whom shoes are a sign of wealth. Others are spectacularly oblivious to the things on their feet, strange constructions of foam and cloth that are a startling departure from the rest of their clothes. In the airport there are back-packing boots and flip-flops, basketball shoes and penny loafers. A business man in trail-running shoes walks by a mother in cowboy boots, all in one place.

Everyone has been taken out of context and put into the same corridors. It is hard to know where they are in their journey. How many flights have they taken so far? Perhaps they have been awake for twenty-four hours with aching knees and bloodshot eyes. Perhaps they have just arrived at the airport, and they are so nervous to fly for the first time that they are nauseous just thinking about it. Everyone is on their way somewhere. The journey is not yet over. Somewhere in the world, a bed with clean sheets is waiting for them to cease their traveling and rest.

10 hours in the Frankfurt Airport

A grey building.

10 hours in the Frankfurt Airport Pt2

Here I sit in concourse B,
ignoring the sticky stains by my feet,
munching banana chips,
and watching Germans walk by
along with the occasional Iranian.
The Germans do not dress like us
(whoever we are)
unless we are German,
in which case our dress
would be remarkably German:
man capris and spunky haircuts.
A man in front of me
is removing his wallet
from his fanny pack.
He is not being ironic.
He is being German.
He efficiently strides off.
His arms are the size of my waist.

De Gaulle Operating System

At Gate B7 you will find
an elderly Algerian couple with kind-eyes
nibbling on overpriced sandwiches. Behind them
you will find clumps and crowds of African Muslims
in long robes and prayer caps, haggard men
surrounded by stout women in hijab. And walking
just behind the well-dressed Muslims you will find
a skinny-legged French woman in a black dress
with a purse far too large for her tiny, toothpick arms.
Follow her up the stairs past
the rich American tourists steeped
in ignorance and privilege,
wearing sweatpants with corporate slogans
plastered across their behinds,
weighed down by shopping bags,
exhibiting all the signs of their psychosis. Stop
at the group of Chinese men who stand,
fashionable, in leather jackets, clearly
craving cigarettes: the world's middle class
with their own destructive habits and self-deceptions.
If you wait long enough you will see pulses of Israelis
moving by in groups with prayer caps and tassels.
And there among the nations, among the many
peoples of the earth, make sure to notice
the clump step of combat boots,
the official orange glint off a reflective backpack,
the walkie-talkie crackling, the straight statements,
straight as a crew cut,

straight as the barrel of a rifle.
It makes one reconsider the building,
the great gray halls and tubes,
twisted cables and wires stretched
along dull, monolithic slabs of cement.
This building is a computer.
The combat boots walk around looking
for zeros and ones in a binary world.
What futility.
They could be sharing a sandwich
with a kind-eyed, elderly Algerian couple.

IX. Germany and Switzerland

Germany and Switzerland

A good friend invited me on a climbing trip to Switzerland. He has family in Germany, the type of family that would give us a place to sleep and then guide us to the boulder field in Switzerland. I was unable to say no.

The Swiss Alps are pristine and green and unreasonably beautiful. The boulder field was hidden up in a mountain gorge that sits in deep shadow for the most of the day. Tall, dark pine trees perch on moss covered boulders next to an alpine brook. The trail system is a treacherous platform of woven roots, which may or may not be hollow underneath, but the rock is sharp and strong, with classic, angular climbs around every other corner. I promptly fell ill, so my climbing was limited, but I had no regrets. Bouldering is a particularly futile sport anyway.

Coincidentally, on our way out of the country, we found ourselves in Stuttgart on the same weekend as Oktoberfest, a fall festival devoted to getting buzzed, glazed, crocked, plastered, wasted, bashed, boozed, liquored, lit, skunked, stewed, inebriated, and drunk. The women wear low-cut *dirndls*, and the men wear tight, leather *lederhosen*, and everyone drinks giant steins of beer, stands on wooden tables, and sings along to John Denver songs. The track-list repeats on a seven song cycle, but no one seems to care, (not even the band) and everyone sings enthusiastically as if they were hearing the song again for the first time. With all the alcohol they were imbibing, they may very well have forgotten by the time the cycle repeats.

The ticket into the tent entitles you to a liter of beer, though that seemed to be only the starting point for most people in the room. The beer is meant to be accompanied by rotisserie chicken, salty and delicious. The bathrooms were crammed full of people evacuating crammed bladders. It is really a bizarre, dehydrating way to spend an evening. I nursed my liter of German beer over the course of a few hours and watched other people appear to enjoy themselves and thought about the fall of the Roman Empire.

After a Flight to Stuttgart

A bitter shot of schnapps
in the evening with chocolate
and a warm wood fire as
the fatigue of travel takes hold
and drags you into the couch,
listening to the guttural hum
of spoken German soothing
you to sleep as they talk
about work in the vineyard
and tomorrow and the current
status of second cousins,
but you don't understand.
You don't speak German.
You are asleep.

Swiss Bahn

On that smooth grey road
we wound through the Alps
and disappeared into mountain tunnels,
braving the false, electric daylight
and the enormous weight of rock
bearing down on those concrete tubes.
It was not the same
seeing the mountains from the inside,
sterile and engineered without
little brown mountain goats
hidden in the pine trees
and villages nestled in each pass,
unashamed in alpine meadows.

Oktoberfest

There is a plastic bag in the air above the fair,
caught up by the wind, sailing above
the cigarette smoke and popcorn.
I try to watch it, spinning in my carnival swing seat,
blinking back the nauseous blood-rush filling
my heavy head with empty space.
The flood lights have blotted out the stars.

After the ride,
back on the ground in the giant tent,
teenagers drunkenly kiss each other
shoulder to shoulder with portly old men
whose lederhosen seem two sizes too tight.
They all stand on wooden benches and sway to the
music,
singing along with the drinking songs.
Prost! The floor is sticky with spilt beer.
Prost! The piss trough runneth over.

Outside, above the sprawling, debauched crowds,
there is a plastic bag floating in the air,
and bright carnival lights flash blue and orange.

Our Uncomfortable, Familiar Love

I have a friend
whose grandfather is fat,
a fine, tight sort of fat
like a well-stuffed chair
and whose grandmother is short
and not skinny
not skinny at all.
They both lived in Germany
but they are not German,
and though they are not funny
not funny in the least,
they give good presents
such fine presents.

X. Kenya

Kenya

I spent the greater portion of my life in Kenya, and yet it is the country least reflected in my poetry. At least, it is not overtly present.

But who can deny that the equatorial sun shining down on the jacaranda trees did not tan my young skin? Or who can say that I did not walk up through thorny scrub-brush to the lip of a dormant volcano to pray to the Creator God? My childhood and Kenya are inexorably linked so that to speak of one is to speak of the other. I was formed as a person there, and that person began to write poetry.

So of course, Kenya is to blame for all of this. Perhaps more poems will come, but for now Kenya is too close to me. I wouldn't be able to write about it well. Those memories will have to mature. Until then, there are only two poems.

I Do Not

I do not begrudge
the night time chuckle
of lions in my memory.
I do not hold my fear against them
when I walked through tall grass
and heard them grunting in the shadows
that guttural lion bark, cat eyes glinting.
I knew there was no promise given
no reasoning, no negotiation,
only hunger and darkness and tiny white stars
in the vast expanse of the night sky,
a dirt path among acacia trees,
a world beyond my control.

Cricket

I learned to play cricket carefully
on the shores of Lake Naivasha.
I was taught by a friendly family
of strangers, British through and through.
We played barefoot, with our flat cricket bats
and balanced wickets amongst acacia trees
that had scattered three inch thorns
like caltrops in the grass. Should
one make a mistaken footstep
the thorn would pierce one's foot
and, just barely, poke out the top.

XI. The South

The South

I used to relate to "the South" largely as an African teenager in exile. I wasn't interested in BBQ, the NCAA, the KKK, or the PCA. I was only interested in returning to Africa. I felt no regional pride. The Appalachians were muted and rounded mountains, simply not the Rockies. Southern history was full of violence, ignorance, and brutality, and I suspected much of it was still festering in the present. I had very few reasons to stay in the South.

Of course, with time I grew to love the shifting of the seasons in the South. I found myself eagerly awaiting the daffodils, dogwoods, and rosebuds of spring. I rejoiced at the crisp fall air, the leaves as brilliant as flames. I found myself voluntarily seeking out blue-grass concerts every Friday night. The deep deciduous woods began to exert their influence on me. I acquired a taste for the opulent fried chicken that various grandmas would make for church potlucks. I was changing.

These poems were brought into being because of two separate journeys. The first was a long drive from Chattanooga, Tennessee to Houston, Texas. As soon as we entered Louisiana, the only music we played was Louis Armstrong. A few dozen trumpet solos later, we were ahead of schedule and decided to spend a couple hours in New Orleans. We ate our *beignets* and did our best to seem street savvy. Then it was onwards over the swampland towards the oil refineries in the desert.

The other trip was a spring break outing by canoe into the Okefenokee swamp of Southern Georgia. The Okefenokee is a peat-bog whose name roughly translates to "Land of the Quivering Earth." It looks like grassland and forest, but it turns out to be miles and miles of black-red water that hosts a thriving alligator population.

My relationship with the South has grown from judgement to love, and yet my affection still includes critique. The world is not yet as it ought to be.

These are poems about Southern places that don't fit into the Chattanooga category. Equally, I could have also called this category, "Two Cities and a Swamp."

City of the Belly

We have taken the tall bridge over the ocean.
We have looked down upon the city
and its satellites glowing distinct
each oil refinery a city unto itself
lit up with a thousand lights on its skyline.
Each is only one machine, too big,
too antisocial to be anything but a bully.
And time to time we see
the flames burning at the tops of smokestacks
like perverted imitations of the sun.
This afternoon we watched the heavy,
rectangular boats float ugly
on the brown, opaque river
carrying oil to the refineries here
in the belly of the empire
where looped tapeworm overpasses
make way for swollen pick-ups.
Is this not our strength?
A people bloated with power.

St. Louis Cathedral

So watch the small brass band before the church,
all swing & swagger on the pavement of the square
where tourists stand agog in cargo shorts, afraid to dance
so overwhelmed by tuba, trumpet, & trombone,
and other sounds of unapologetic life.
These braggarts of vitality with black skin
sweating as their instruments shout & blare
& suddenly the pallor of our middle class existence
shows itself as pale, an imitation:
the sad and glowing screens,
the self-imposed slavery to self, the bondage
to a studio's imagination: making mecca
 to Disney World each year,
& we find ourselves ashamed before
 the shoe-shine hustler &
the blue-grass busker, they who
sit in judgment over us,
who kneel down close
to all the dirt and grime that coats the street.
& we are shamed by each contrary story which
reveals our comfort as a lie, an enemy of life.
For sure as death we will be brought down low
& be made weak, we will taste poverty & sickness.
But even now we will not dance or play or sweat.
for we prefer to watch this life than live it.

Okefenokee

We move on the red-black water of the swamp,
dark whirlpools spinning off our paddles then
trailing in the wake of borrowed canoes,
mile by watery mile, pulling on the paddle
through wide swamp prairies of grass and sky,
through swaths of char-burnt apocalyptic spikes,
the remains of pine trees lost to flames,
burnt black down to the very edge of the water.

There are few good omens here, almost none.
It is a place of great foreboding
watched over by the long, cunning reptile faces
of guardian alligators, lying still in the sunshine,
dangerous in every snakelike sinew
with their rough ridged backs, regular as saw-teeth.

This is a land without land,
a land of quivering earth and floating grass,
where still water suddenly ripples with unknown intent,
where quick-moving clouds shift across the sky,
where the sun-burnt bald heads of vultures patrol,
circling wide and slow above the swamp,
where a freezing wind comes rushing in at night,
each gust loud approaching from the north.

The bog land holds its secrets close
mulling, digesting, rotting underneath, yet
even here the white bright heron springs up
sharp and straight into the blue sky,
even the claustrophobic myrtle bushes
open up onto acres of shining lily pads,
and single yellow flowers grow
floating distinct and tiny on the black water.

XII. Miscellaneous

Miscellaneous

Some poems don't have a clear category. They are not tied to a place or theme. They were not forged in the furnace of new experiences that travel generates. They do not reflect on a life lived before God. What holds them together as a category is that they don't have a clear category. They exist, and that is enough.

These poems are probably best understood as products of the imagination, though one must readily admit that no human poet creates *ex nihilo*. What we call creation could be more accurately described as combination, word to word and idea to idea. Our imaginations do the combining, but they too are shaped by outside forces. So it follows that we ought to be careful about what we allow to shape our imaginations.

I aspire to an imagination shaped by poetry and liturgy, by old stories and the wise dead, by wilderness and wry humor. Of course the real list would likely include sitcoms, advertisements, and video games, influences which do not bestow any sense of depth or nobility upon me, though I certainly would prefer to appear deep and noble.

As it turns out, we do not have complete control over what shapes our imaginations. We can't pre-screen the stories we hear. We can't approach all forms of media with fear and trembling at what it might do to us. But we can return again and again to the stories we know are good.

Whatever the shape of my imagination may be, it appears I was concerning myself with emperors and slugs, not to mention geese, elephants, and Brazilian jiu-jitsu instructors. Feel free to concern yourself, also, with these things.

Unaccustomed

I am unaccustomed to meeting emperors
so I shall drink my tea alone
and not heed the call of the herald
who stands pounding at my front door.
The emperor can wait for another day.
Today I prefer to take my tea alone.

The Wrong Person

The wrong person never could be right.
He only takes left turns,
inevitably circling back on himself.
The wrong person failed first grade,
again and again,
and now sits as an eighteen year old
in a tiny seat, with stubble on his chin,
tracing capital letters on wide-lined paper.
The wrong person's car broke down.
His cat died.
He caught liver cancer
which isn't even contagious.
His refrigerator is empty
save for an unopened jar of mayonnaise.

Pinocchio

It was always tough for Pinocchio
starting again at a new school,
his joints well-oiled and
his wooden face well-polished
to put his best clog-shod foot forward.
To be sure, it was a disability.
Not being a real boy made it difficult
to make to new friends,
so he sat inside at recess
slumped over on his desk
while all the other children played outside.
I don't know what you can do for a puppet
who has severed all his strings.

The Slug

Consider the slug, you automatons.
It does not strive or toil.
It is not ambitious or busy.
The slug does as the slug is.
It eats the edges of leaves
and slimes to and fro, living
in the cool shadows of the garden.
Be like the slug.
Consider the grace of the world
even for small and slimy things.

Aunt Irma

The plaid pantsuit blended
so well with the plaid couches
that Aunt Irma became a chameleon
and we lost sight of her
among the ugly basement furniture.
For all we know, she is still down there,
foraging for butterscotch candy
between the couch cushions.

Poetry is Cheap

Poetry is cheap
if love is cheap,
and we all know,
ladies and gentlemen,
that love is not cheap.
It costs you your life.

All This Juice and Joy

It was the gauche part of town
every building gaudy and tottering,
leaning against each other like dominoes,
florid carnival colors mismatched
on door-frames and windowsills.
Oh, but the people had vigor
leaping up to meet each new day
already sweating as the sun rose,
pushing their banana carts
and peddling ice-cream coolers.
Every child dancing in the street
or pounding rhythms from drums.
The trees bled sticky sap
that smelled of bitter licorice
but in the evening the old men
still gathered around underneath
the whorled and gnarled branches
to practice their elocution
and tell the same stories
once more, only this time
grander, with the heroism
more enunciated, pronounced.
And when the sun set
the whole neighborhood
would flicker with shadows
from candles lit in the windows
and street fires on the corners
where the people gathered

to roast meat and sing.
The nights were warm,
and even a long life
was much too short.

Not Quite

The poem is, somehow,
incomplete. It lacks confidence
with its
linebreaks?
Or it confuses them
with being poetic,
so
it
trails
one
ordinary
word
after
another
without any real reason or
emphasis,
just taking up space on the page.

It does not squint or spit.
There are missed opportunities
to suckle, fracture, and soothe.
Under the false pretense of a rhyme
it wastes the reader's precious ~~time~~
seconds.

There are no characters.
There is no setting.
There are only disembodied words
that never become flesh,
never suffer and die,
never rise from the grave.
They float, abstract and pristine,
sure to never sully themselves
by touching a human soul
or worse,
a body.

It is a poem
written about poetry,
like a snake
eating its own tail
until it disappears.

The Mall

One does not expect, when entering the mall
to come across a Brazilian jiujitsu dojo
or the master of that dojo
grabbing you by the collar
and slamming you to the ground
for advertising.

One Never Learns the Steps

"Dance" they said
"Dance, elephant boy,"
but only the young dance,
and those who remember are always old,
wrinkled gray with large ears
and drooping noses dragging
on the ground, ivory dentures
fizzing in their nightly nap,
a stumbling dance into
the kitchen when they can't sleep.
In fact, the old are always dancing.
How else to forget?

After Finding a Goose Nest

What is it to have children?
Does the goose wonder at the eggs she lays
and surrounds with downy feathers?
Each child comes blinking
and burping into this world,
unable to even support the weight
of its own head, fingers clasped
on whatever they can clasp.
Tiny bright eyes and downy hair.
It is something to be small,
with soft feet, unsuited for walking.
Still without the monumental achievement
of language, by which we shape our thoughts.
Thoughts, which inevitably lead us back to love.
Love which, again, brings more children
stretching and grimacing into our common life,
each child a helpless source of hope.
Welcome.

Lilacs Grow in her Footsteps

Lilacs grow in her footsteps
sprouting all up and down the coastal roads
spilling purple onto the hillsides.
These are the legacies we leave:
the apple trees and lavender,
the overgrown copse of pine
that shelters the rogue woodchuck,
the stone fences pieced together,
slightly taller every year
after the spring plowing
dredges up new stones.
There was an old house here
but now only the chimney stands
and everywhere there are lilacs

lilacs

lilacs

lilacs.

Living Under Water

You can't.

XIII. Grief

Grief

Poetry is a preparation for death, and death is the ever-present companion of poetry.

Many people get along just fine without poetry. But when tragedy strikes, when the tire crosses the yellow line, when the cells in our lungs turn cancerous, we go looking for words to give us meaning, to encourage us, and to give us hope for the dawn. Poetry does that for us. It does not stop death. It does not even delay it. Poetry watches death come and, seeking to tell us the truth, says, "This is natural. Do not be afraid." But immediately after saying that, poetry goes on to shake us and yell, "It should not be this way. Deny death. Do not go gently." Poetry holds these two stances in tension. Truthfully, it can be no other way.

And when death does come, as it always inevitably does, to take the ones we love away, before finally taking us, poetry gives us space to grieve. Because, natural or not, each death is a tragedy. Each loss is the source of a deep suffering in the human soul, one that cannot be consoled until the loved one is returned. We must not ignore that suffering. We must give voice to our grief, or we will be consumed. We must watch for resurrection.

Minnesota

So even the simple things will fade away
like falling into sleep, and let us mourn
that rest can be a lonely comfort. Soft
and still, our breath, to steal a little life
like cookies from the jar: sweet oatmeal sin.
The everlasting summer sunset dims,
though all the kids were long since sent to bed,
pajama shirts and wet blonde hair, to fall
asleep, hands cool beneath their pillows. Rugs
and cards and birthday poem theater
so even the simple things will fade away
to gold or gray. Split pine, roast beef, and joy;
in loss there is no good advice to give,
no toast or cereal to start the day.
The quiet only, just an empty seat.
I cut the grass again with pine sap stains
on khaki pants, awaiting lunch, some roast
beef stew with bread. And so our time will come.
With rest and love and humble sweat, and knead
this life like dough. How patient love is sad.
For even the simple things will fade away.

www.ingramcontent.com/pod-product-compliance
Lightning Source LLC
Chambersburg PA
CBHW032033040426
42449CB00007B/879